labyrinth

landscape of the soul

Di Williams

Copyright © 2009 Di Williams

Published 2011, reprinted 2012, 2018

Wild Goose Publications

21 Carlton Court, Glasgow G5 9JP, UK. www.ionabooks.com

Wild Goose Publications is the publishing division of the Iona Community.

Scottish Charity No. SC003794. Limited Company Reg. No. SC096243.

ISBN 978-1-84952-185-7

Design by James Hartigan.

Overseas distribution:

Australia: Willow Connection Pty Ltd, Unit 4A, 3-9 Kenneth Road,
Manly Vale, NSW 2093.

New Zealand: Pleroma, Higginson Street, Otane 4170, Central Hawkes Bay

Canada: Novalis/Bayard Publishing & Distribution, 10 Lower Spadina Ave.
Suite 400, Toronto, Ontario M5V 2Z2.

Printed by Bell & Bain, Thornliebank, Glasgow, Scotland.

Cover picture – Maggie's Centre Labyrinth, Dundee, Scotland.

WILD GOOSE PUBLICATIONS
THE IONA COMMUNITY

www.ionabooks.com

labyrinth

landscape of the soul

Awake my soul

Psalm 57:8

WALK THIS PATH
WITH AN OPEN HEART + MIND
SEEKING AWARENESS
AS YOU

Trinity Gardens Labyrinth, Whitehaven, England.

Introduction

When I discovered my first labyrinth in 1993 in Threecliffs Bay, South Wales, it was one of only a relatively small number of labyrinths in the British Isles. Out of the blue, I had come across an ancient tool which proved significant in caring for my whole self, body, mind and spirit.

From that moment on the beauty of these ancient circular patterns on the ground captivated me. I discovered that walking them offered a calming of the mind, a nurturing for my soul as well as a healthy bit of gentle exercise!

In the last few years the number of labyrinths being built across the planet has expanded rapidly.

In the UK we are seeing the beginning of a similar growth in construction and use. They are being installed and used in schools, colleges, universities, hospices, urban parks, private and public gardens, spirituality and retreat centres, religious settings, city centre streets, woodland, beaches and many more sites.

The design is popping up in new places such as in circular rugs, on the cover of best selling novels, in pieces of fine and land art, on CD covers, crafted into musical instruments such as Sting's lute and as a mould through which molten chocolate flows in a TV advert!

As more people in the UK are discovering labyrinths near where they live, this straightforward practical guide explains what labyrinths are and shows how a growing number of organisations, groups and individuals are using them. But this book is not simply a practical guide. It charts a personal journey of discovery and awakening. It is a book for the soul.

I hope the photography and words capture the calming beauty of these ancient yet new paths so that in picking up the book you experience a moment of peace or personal reflection.

Saltburn Beach Labyrinth, England.

I carry a deeper hope, that through your encounter with this book you may be persuaded, in the gentlest possible way, to find your way to and through a labyrinth, and maybe, one sunny day on a deserted beach, to make your own!

First step

As far back as I can remember I have
sought an inner place of silence.

Through the beauty of a spring time
mountain walk, the quiet, early
morning slipping of an open canoe
across a misty lake, the night wander
under a star-full sky, sometimes an
awareness of something other has
been awakened. In those moments I
feel connected with and merged into
a wider consciousness, in which I
experience enveloping love and
deep, deep peace and joy.

I have learned not to expect such
experiences. They cannot be forced or
earned. They are simply given. As wind
blowing through trees they leave their
whisper of presence and are gone.

Finding a simple way to quieten my
busy mind has always helped me be
receptive to the subtle stirring of my
soul. Coming across the existence of
this ancient path for reflection called
a labyrinth has been the discovery of
a very special way of doing this.

Mercy Centre Labyrinth, Burlingame, US.

"To a mind that is still the
whole universe surrenders"

Chuang Tzu

Rounding a headland on the coastal path of the Gower Peninsula my attention was caught by a circular shaped pattern lying in the river valley below where the grass, stone and sand met.

I made my way past the wild ponies and down the cliff to the entrance of what looked at first to be a spiral trail formed from the natural elements in which it lay. It drew me in. Walking through it intrigued me. I loved its simple beauty but didn't connect it with anything more than an enjoyable wander.

I didn't realise that the path I had just walked was part of a history of labyrinth-making that reached back over 4000 years. Neither did I realise on that beautiful spring day that I had begun a journey that would lead to a discovery of the richness of the labyrinth as a means of nourishing the human soul.

Threecliffs Bay Labyrinth, Gower Peninsula, Wales.

"Very seldom do you come upon a space...when you may stop and simply be. Or wonder who, after all, you are."

Ursula K LeGuin

"Unwinding and path finding...a beautiful space in the turning world"

Helen, Edinburgh Labyrinth

Threecliffs Bay Labyrinth, Wales.

It was several years later before I encountered my second labyrinth. I was visiting St Martin's College, Lancaster where there is a simple replica of the medieval Chartres Cathedral Labyrinth painted on the ground outside the college chapel. Discovering that a labyrinth workshop was on offer, I decided to go and see what labyrinths were all about.

The labyrinth itself had been painted on tarmac in white paint. It wasn't particularly well made. You could see where some of the lines had been wrongly drawn and an attempt had been made to erase the mistakes. It wasn't the most beautiful of labyrinths but it became an important one in my personal journey.

After an introduction to their history, the workshop facilitator invited each one of us to enter the labyrinth. Just before I stepped in, the facilitator invited me to reflect on the question 'What do you seek?' That particular question proved timely.

I walked the winding but unswerving path to the circle's centre, taking time there to be still and reflect. Somehow the act of walking quietened me. The walk became almost a physical meditation. I left the labyrinth with greater clarity and a deeper sense of integration with the various aspects of my life.

Since then I have encountered labyrinths in many countries and cultures. I have worked with others in creating sand labyrinths on river banks and by the ocean, leaf labyrinths in parkland, a seven circuit classical labyrinth painted on cloth, a limestone labyrinth in a clearing of trees on a Yorkshire Dales hillside and a beautiful stone replica of the Chartres Medieval Labyrinth in an eighteenth century garden in the heart of the University of Edinburgh, Scotland.

I have helped to create these circles of reflection as a resource for all who might have a need to seek an ancient yet new place for the soul's nourishing.

"There is **nothing so wise** as a circle."

Rainer Maria Rilke

"...We give thanks for **places of simplicity** and peace. Let us find such a place within ourselves. We give thanks for places of **refuge and beauty.** Let us find such a place within ourselves... We give thanks for places of nature's truth and freedom, of **joy, inspiration and renewal,** places where all creatures may find acceptance and belonging.

Let us search for these places: in the world, in ourselves and in others. Let us **restore** them. Let us strengthen and protect them and **let us create them.** May we mend this outer world according to the truth of our inner life and **may our souls be shaped and nourished** by nature's eternal wisdom..."

Michael Leunig

Columba's Bay Labyrinth, Isle of Iona, Scotland.

Potted history

Labyrinths have been known to the human race for well over 4000 years. They seem to have emerged and re-emerged, capturing our interest in several time waves and in slightly differing forms throughout this period.

Classical

There is evidence of the existence of the classical labyrinth symbol (the most ancient labyrinth pattern) across southern Europe and North Africa from roughly 2000 BCE. Over time it took the form of rock carvings and paintings, inscriptions on ceramics, tiles and coins. The same basic design began to appear across Asia, the Americas and Southern Africa in an assortment of forms including rock carvings, sand games, wall paintings, wooden sculptures and woven baskets.

Roman

Somewhere between c165 BCE-400 CE the classical design morphed into that of the more complex Roman one. The Roman labyrinths were mainly mosaic pavement labyrinths laid in the floors of bathhouses, villas and tombs throughout the Roman Empire. Virtually all such mosaics were too small for walking.

In Britain there are several known examples of Roman labyrinth mosaic pavements such as the Harpham mosaic (Hull and East Riding Museum) and the mosaic from the Roman site at Caerleon in Newport, Gwent, now in the Caerleon Museum.

Medieval

The medieval period marked a new wave of labyrinth building as well as a significant development in labyrinth design. Towards the end of the 9th century a monk called Otfrid took the classical seven-circuit labyrinth pattern and added four extra circuits creating the more complex eleven-circuit labyrinth design we know today as the medieval labyrinth.

His drawing in the endpaper of his Book of Gospels became a precedent for the construction of dozens of 12th-13th century labyrinths found in cathedrals and churches across Europe. As time went on, breaks or turns in the walls at north, south, east and west points were added to the pattern.

The most famous medieval labyrinth of this type, the Chartres Labyrinth, laid down in c1201, is still intact in the floor of the nave of Chartres Cathedral, France. It is probably the most walked labyrinth in the world.

Indeed, these labyrinths were built precisely for walking. They offered a bounded space for personal reflection and spiritual pilgrimage. The later classical and medieval stone or turf labyrinths of Northern Europe, largely laid down between the 12th and 17th centuries, were also walking labyrinths.

Contemporary

It is against this long history of shifting design and use that the contemporary revival of interest in labyrinths has blossomed.

Perhaps, as some suggest, there is something in the collective unconscious of the earth community of the late twentieth and early twenty-first centuries that recognises a need for unique spaces like labyrinths.

Labyrinths seem to have emerged again at a time when we need help in recovering a more balanced, reflective and inclusive way of living together on this planet.

So what is a labyrinth?

We have seen that a labyrinth is an ancient pattern, an archetypal image that has been passed down through generations and cultures as a form of reflective tool.

Over the last thousand years or so these fascinating patterns have most often been constructed as pathways on the ground big enough for us to enter and walk.

The classical, Roman and medieval designs have one path only. Unlike the later development of mazes with their many dead ends and constant choice of paths, walking the one simple and winding path of a labyrinth has the potential to help us release and quieten our mind. We don't have to think where we go next. We don't have to think at all! We just place one foot in front of the other and walk.

Slowly walking the single path, step by step, to the centre of the labyrinth, enjoying the space at the centre and then retracing the same path back out, gives enough time to unwind and let go of everyday concerns in order to renew some sense of inner calm, balance and perspective.

In the fast-paced world in which we now live, we need simple, beautiful places like labyrinths that draw us in by the attraction of their pattern to slow ourselves down, still the busy mind and connect us again with our deep inner resources.

Columba's Bay Labyrinth, Isle of Iona, Scotland.

"Solvitur ambulando"
(It is solved by walking)

St Augustine of Hippo

Walking
a labyrinth

When you come across a labyrinth
for the first time it might be good to
be aware of one or two things that
can help you relax into the walk.

Before you step onto the path take
a moment to become aware of your
breathing and your consciousness of
being in the present moment. Although
there is no right or wrong way to walk
a labyrinth, your first experience is
a unique event. Many people find
that being as open in heart and mind
as they can, with no agenda or
expectation of how the walk may
be for them, is most valuable.

What is important is simply
to acknowledge the experience
that is yours.

Braemore Mizmaze, Turf Labyrinth, England.

"Let us pause from thinking…
let us stop the noise. In the
silence let us listen to our hearts"

Michael Leunig

Releasing

When you are ready to enter the labyrinth gently focus on taking one step at a time. You may find that your mind is swilling with thoughts. If possible, acknowledge what is preoccupying you and then, during the time you walk the path from the entrance to the centre of the labyrinth, try to let go of these immediate concerns and give your inner self a sense of spaciousness.

Sometimes the old thoughts creep back to preoccupy you as you move along the path. Note them and try leaving them with the physical step you are making. Breathe in the present moment and take the next step in openness again. Often this opportunity to release pressing thoughts and feelings allows new insights and intuitions to emerge.

Receiving

Give yourself time in the centre of the labyrinth to be aware of your feelings and thoughts and to receive what is there for you in that moment.

Returning

As you return along the same path you walked in on, reflect on what it is you might take away from this experience. A tool like a labyrinth allows you to work with, and integrate, your intellectual and intuitive selves. After you leave the labyrinth you may want to take a moment to reflect on what it was you thought and felt as you journeyed.

Some practical details may enhance your time in the labyrinth. Throughout the walk it may help to keep an inner focus that is just peripherally aware of the presence of others on the path.

If someone is walking very slowly ahead of you, and you feel your rhythm wants to be quicker, take the initiative to move around and ahead of them. Go the pace your body wants to go, remembering to have respect for the journey of others.

You may find that as you walk the single path towards the centre, other walkers are returning from the centre on their way out. Keep your eye on the path you are on and be prepared to weave around the person before continuing your journey in. You may find yourself sharing the centre with others already there. Stand, sit, or even lie down if you wish to and there is enough room. Use the labyrinth in the way that is supportive for you.

To step into

a labyrinth

...is a kind of homecoming

Reflections from the labyrinth

Tibetan bells

I had been invited to join a small group of women in walking a labyrinth in the bush of New South Wales. The labyrinth lay beneath wonderful eucalyptus trees in a slightly raised area looking out to the surrounding hills. The path was a dusty pink and red, the colour of the earth in which it lay. It was a winter day, sharp and bright with the long shadows of the afternoon sun. It all looked and smelled so good.

Whilst walking the labyrinth I remembered that I had a small container of coloured sand in my pocket that had come from a Mandala, a meditative sand design, created by the Tashi Lhunpo monks who had made a recent visit to Edinburgh with the Dalai Lama.

In Edinburgh the monks had chanted and blessed the earth in preparation for the building of the Edinburgh Labyrinth. Before they left for their journey home they had dispersed the Mandala and given me some of the sand to take away. It was usual to disperse the sand in running water but I decided to take mine to Australia to share with my friend there.

Walking this beautiful bush labyrinth I sprinkled a few grains of the sand at the points where I had been reflecting. It was in the sharing of experience with the other walkers afterwards that I realised more connections than I could imagine had taken place on the labyrinth.

One of the women in the group, who was in the early stages of recovery from a debilitating illness, spoke about how she had worried before she had entered the labyrinth that she would not be strong enough to manage the walk. She did and said "I felt much better after I'd finished. What I couldn't understand is why I kept hearing Tibetan bells as I walked."

Rachum Labyrinth, Canberra, Australia.

The labyrinth lay beneath wonderful eucalyptus trees in a slightly raised area looking out to the surrounding hills. The path was a dusty pink and red, the colour of the earth in which it lay.

"**Nothing in all creation is so like God as stillness.**"

Meister Eckhart

Inviting the bell

"May the sound of this bell penetrate deeply into the cosmos. In even the darkest spots, may living beings hear it clearly so their suffering will cease, understanding arise in their hearts, and they can transcend the path of anxiety and sorrow."

Thich Nhat Hanh

"Cease seeing with the mind
and see with the vital spirit."

Chuang Tzu

Trinity Gardens Labyrinth, Whitehaven, England.

An open heart

The secret of walking the labyrinth is to walk with no expectation but with an openness of heart, mind and soul.

All labyrinth walks are different. One day the walk will be nothing more than pleasant exercise; the next walk may offer a new insight, realisation or transforming experience. A walk in the labyrinth can enable the individual to connect with their deepest motivations and meanings, their 'spiritual' self.

For some their experience of walking this path may provide a container for encounter with what is most important or sacred in their life. For others it may simply provide a place of peace.

According to the Rev Dr Lauren Artress, a leader within the contemporary labyrinth movement, the labyrinth is always "a mirror for the soul".

One step at a time...

Jean's story

For me, the labyrinth seems to be different things at different times. Some days, it's 'just a pleasant walk'. On other days, it can be a much more powerful and profound experience.

I was walking one day, in the midst of some very difficult work-related issues - unpleasant relationships, hostility between staff, and a lack of direction within the organisational unit.
I was walking quite fast, carrying the tension, anger and frustration with me. I was impatient to complete the walk.

As I recognised this, I also realised that I was looking ahead all the time, tracing the path with my eyes - "where do I go next, and after the next curve, where then? And then?"

Suddenly, I realised I didn't need to worry. I didn't need to know where the next corner was or what might be round it. I just needed the faith to put one foot in front of the other, and trust that I would eventually get there - wherever 'there' might be. I slowed down, and enjoyed the rest of the walk.

A few days later, and quite by chance, I came across a quote from Martin Luther King Jr. which summed up that moment for me.

The Edinburgh Labyrinth, Scotland.

"To take the first step in faith, you don't need to see the whole staircase; just take the first step."

Martin Luther King Jr

The Edinburgh Labyrinth, University of Edinburgh, Scotland.

Seeing differently...

Tim's story

Coming from a Quaker background, I like things that encourage thinking for yourself, spirituality that doesn't shove anything down your throat and ways of encouraging calm and peace. Nevertheless, I'll admit I didn't quite get how walking around in circles would help me do this.

Still, one afternoon, on a revision break from the library, an acquaintance and I decided that we'd walk the new labyrinth in George Square. I took the lead. Walking around the edge I felt a little silly, but then going round and round I began to stop thinking of anything else, just the lines and following them round, only occasionally interrupted by passing my fellow walker.

After a few minutes' circling I reached the middle and stopped and looked out, suddenly feeling very calm. I turned to my friend, who was following soon after, and it was as if we were very close, and had known each other a long time, despite that not being the case. We looked around the Square, as if surveying the view having climbed a mountain and it looked somehow different.

But most strange of all was coming out again. Neither of us could bear to cut across the lines. We walked back out again the way we came in, stepped out of the labyrinth, and sat down on the bench at the side. Very calm now, we entered into a long conversation, learning about each other's lives.

"When you get into that state of mind – you know the one, where you see everything in slow motion and you can hear the blood in your ears – you know there's something more to all of this."

Vienna, Greenbelt Festival

Unblocking the mind…

Heather's story

I wasn't really sure what to expect, perhaps just an opportunity to be peaceful, to still the endless chatter of my mind, perhaps, to leave the worries of the world behind for half an hour or so! I didn't realise that many of the things I had been reading or thinking about recently would come into the labyrinth with me, to be worked on, as I walked.

I have felt recently and for some time now, like I don't have enough time. I am always running late, getting up early enough and then finding half an hour has just disappeared and I don't know what happened to it… like my time has been stretched thin. In the labyrinth, everything seemed to slow down and "reset" itself. Although I was only in the labyrinth for about 20 minutes, it was a FULL 20 minutes, not thin, if that makes any sense.

Winding my way out of the labyrinth, I didn't realise that I was at the end until I came around the last twist and saw the exit. I was horrified! I didn't want to leave. Strangely…I felt safe standing upon it, as if it was wrapped in a force field that nothing could penetrate.

I felt lighter on my feet afterwards as I walked away and felt "full", refuelled with a need to do something positive in this world.

I have been feeling very "stuck" in many ways, personally, spiritually and academically. The next day, I stopped trying to read or write, I got online, got on the phone, made some new contacts and am off to do some research in the field.

Grace Cathedral Labyrinth, San Francisco, US.

"It is difficult today to leave one's friends and family and deliberately practise the art of solitude, for an hour or a day or a week. And yet, when it is done, I find there is a quality to being alone that is incredibly precious. Life rushes back into the void, richer, more vivid, fuller than before."

Anne Morrow Lindbergh

Freedom of spirit

A friend and I arrived at Edinburgh Prison nearly an hour before the labyrinth session we were going to facilitate was due to start. However, we hadn't taken into consideration the time it would take to check our identity, divest us of any form of electronic communication and lock us through a series of corridors and doors till we eventually got into the Chapel itself. Having started to feel quite shut in, it felt good to arrive in a more open space where we could lay out the canvas labyrinth.

We introduced ourselves to the men who turned up for the session and talked a little about how labyrinths are places where we can connect with our sorrows and joys. When it was time to walk the labyrinth, the men were invited to sit for a while and then in their own time and at their own pace to enter and start walking the path. All but one walked the labyrinth that day.

Afterwards we drank tea and coffee and chatted quite openly. As I listened to their stories I was reminded again that labyrinths are reflectors of what is happening within us. We cannot determine what experience we will have on a labyrinth, only enter with an open heart and mind without expectation of what it might be. The range of possibility was aptly illustrated that day by two personal reflections.

One man told us that feelings about his sister's suicide, which had happened while he had been inside, had come flooding up for him as he walked. Up till then he had not really connected with the reality of her tragic death. The labyrinth had provided a contained, safe space within which he had felt a different quality of inner freedom to remember and reflect. It had been a significant and healing experience for him.

Just as importantly, a fellow inmate described his experience as merely "a wee, gentle stroll". Within the confines of the prison that was no simple gift.

A child's peace

I stood at the entrance to a canvas labyrinth which we had laid down for the long Bank Holiday weekend at a Christian Music and Arts Festival. There were thousands of people on site busily milling from one workshop, concert or talk to the next one. We too had been inundated with people of all ages queuing to walk the labyrinth.

A girl aged about seven approached the entrance where I stood. I had begun to recognise a few people who were returning to walk the labyrinth for a second time and her face was familiar. I asked her if she had walked earlier in the weekend. She had. "Tell me, why have you come back to walk again?" I enquired. "For the peace," she replied, "I just love the peace."

Child's reflection after walking the Greenbelt Festival Labyrinth.

"It is such a **great experience** to walk through a labyrinth following your feet and in the middle to **get rid of your worries** and come back out with none at all!"

Alys (10)

Beneath the stone

The winter dawn chill hung in the air as I approached the centre of the labyrinth. I began the walk in simple openness of heart and mind, aware of letting go of conscious thoughts of the day ahead of me as they arose and focusing instead on each step on the path I was making, breathing in, attentive to the present moment, slowing my mind down to become more sensitive to the movement of my spirit. I could hear only the call of birds and the distant rumble of traffic.

In the centre of the labyrinth was a large standing stone of green-grey serpentine. As I completed my walk in and stepped into the centre circle I reached out to place my hand on the stone as I had done on many walks before. Usually I enjoyed the still, solid, grounded feel of the rock... it helped me drop more readily into my own sense of centredness and stillness as I sought to prepare for the day that lay ahead. This morning it was very different.

As my fingers made contact I felt the icy cold of winter stone on flesh. Then, as if in an instant, my usual boundaries of perception dissolved.

I plummeted downwards, down below the stone cold rock, down through the earth's chilled crust, down, down towards the core of the earth itself. I sensed the impending inferno and immediately was caught up in the molten heat at the planet's core. I was at the heart of this living organism's life. Then all I could feel was searing heat and all I could see was blazing fire as it roared up and up through dense layers of rock, up to the cold, winter earth beneath the centre stone till it burst up through the rock I was touching and everything was subsumed in light and heat.

As quickly as the experience arrived it left me.

I stood in the labyrinth's centre, my hand on ice-cold rock, slightly shaking, aware that I felt connected to the inner landscape of the physical earth in a way that would for ever alter my sense of relationship with its dynamic and immensely potent life force.

The early morning sun finally broke through the grey mist as I returned along the same path. Only, I was changed.

Mercy Centre Labyrinth, Burlingame, US.

Across cultures

I was staying in a fishing village on the west coast of Morocco. When the tide was out there was a wide beach peopled with women in burkhas paddling up to their ankles, men and children in bathers splashing and swimming.

One afternoon I decided to draw a seven-circuit classical labyrinth in the sand. I found a long stick and took my time laying the pattern out with the entrance facing the sea. When I finished I stuck the stick in the sand by the entrance to the path, stepped into the labyrinth and took the time I wanted to enjoy the walk.

I half noticed a small group of young boys, around ten years old, watching me as I drew the pattern in the sand. Now as I finished my walk and moved away I watched them enter the labyrinth one after another. One carried a surfboard almost as big as he was under his arm. They half walked half ran around the path, occasionally shouting words to each other in Arabic.

One of the boys started to scrub out the lines in the sand with his feet.

As he did so, one of his friends got my stick from the entrance and very carefully started to fill in the pattern again. I was fascinated by his care as he painstakingly re-worked the lines.

As the boys eventually came out of the labyrinth I took my camera to photograph it close up. The self assumed guardian, still with the stick, ran towards me to stop me and make me understand he wanted me to wait for a moment. With the stick he drew a large heart in front of the entrance to the path and below it a word in Arabic. Then he shouted to the others and they all ran back in to let me photograph them in the labyrinth.

It wasn't till I got back to the UK and checked that I realised he had written the Arabic word for labyrinth above the heart.

Essaouria Beach Labyrinth, Morocco.

Spiritual reflection

We have seen that people seek out labyrinths for personal reflection. It is a way of giving themselves the opportunity, for a short while, to move out of the regular ebb and flow of life and step into a space that can somehow act as a container for their sorrows and joys, questions and hopes.

Although labyrinths may be walked for a variety of reasons, such as simply giving oneself space in the day to slow down or focus on a particular issue, for many people, walking a labyrinth is a regular spiritual practice. Whether they are Buddhist or Christian, Muslim or Jew, Hindu or Sikh, Baha'i or Shaman the labyrinth is a path of welcome. It is a path for all.

Perhaps most significantly in this time of our planet's history, the labyrinth is proving to be a place where all can explore the meanings and motivations of their inner life and find resources for their own journey. Many today would claim no religious connection but are aware of their own need to nourish their soul as well as their mind and body. The labyrinth is a unique place where people of diverse beliefs and lifestyles walk a common path together.

"In a world of electronic beeps and tunes it is silence after all that feeds the soul. Turn off the machines, **embrace the chattering mind that follows in their wake** and walk along gently into a stillness, a space for peace. "

Beach Labyrinth Tangalooma Island, Australia.

"Step by step...silence moves more quietly now
or is it I who move within the core of space and
stillness as I turn from where I stand to where
I aim for. It is not far. And yet it's further than I've
ever been before, although in truth I know it.
Or did I dream of shores, of timeless shores
where safely shoes and socks are shed
and feet encounter paths of richest being.
Step by step silence moves more quietly now
as I in awe, approach the place, the peace,
I'll never find, except the labyrinth direct me,
step by step, in silence."

The Labyrinth by Lynne Chitty

Walking the path together

Walking a labyrinth with a group can be very different from enjoying a personal reflective walk alone. Some groups use the labyrinth as a space for ritual or ceremony.

Recently a group of young men who had just graduated from university were seen to walk into the university labyrinth, each proudly carrying a red scroll box with their degree certificate inside. Maybe one or other had walked the labyrinth before or perhaps it was the first time in a labyrinth for all these students. Whatever their history, this day they were consciously (or unconsciously) using the labyrinth as a place of marking and celebrating an important occasion and transition in their lives.

On a special birthday weekend I drew a labyrinth in the sand of a Scottish beach. I was given a birthday cake to carry into the centre. My family, friends and Zed the dog followed me into the centre and when everyone had arrived, we sang 'happy birthday' and ate the cake!

I have worked with groups who have walked the labyrinth together to mark the coming of winter, intentionally share a journey alongside those of very different faiths, or commemorate 9/11 with a walk for peace.

There are endless possibilities for creating meaningful ritual or ceremonial walks together.

"To return to the present is to be in contact with life. Life can only be found in the present moment, because the past no longer is and the future has not yet come...liberation, awakening, peace, joy, and happiness can only be found in the present moment. The place of our appointment is right here, in this very place...

Life is not a particular place or destination. Life is a path."

Thich Nhat Hanh

Ritual fire, group walk on Scargill Labyrinth, England.

Children & labyrinths

Labyrinths attract children.

They want to follow the path to the centre, excited by the task of getting there! The energy they bring to the path is usually marked by vitality and fun! Children on the path run, jump, hop, walk backwards as well as walk it in the most usual way, step by step to the centre and back. They have an innate knowledge that there is no right or wrong way to follow the path of a labyrinth…only the way it feels good to move along it.

Children often seem to connect with creation and life around them in an immediately intuitive way. They don't quite have the social or spiritual barriers that adults sometimes experience. On the labyrinth children can remind us of things that are important.

Mirehouse Heather Labyrinth, Cumbria, England.

Julian's Bower Turf Labyrinth, Alkborough, England

"A young girl running, skipping with joy and wonder, energy and life."

Discovering labyrinths

Norwich Cathedral Labyrinth, England.

"A welcome break
for a tired traveller."

Lynn, Canadian visitor, Edinburgh Labyrinth

Decoration & fine art

The labyrinth pattern is evident in paintings and decorative work throughout the last few thousand years. It continues to hold an attraction for artists.

Walking into a village art show in Yorkshire I spotted a simple cream felt cloak. On closer inspection the information suggested it had been made for someone who practised an indigenous Shamanic spirituality. What drew me to the cloak was the splendid labyrinth the artist had embroidered across the back of the garment.

I was reminded that the labyrinth circle is an archetypal image of wholeness and unity as well as being a symbol of journeying.

In 2006 a fine arts student at the Edinburgh College of Art set up an installation, 'Reflective Paths', in the University of Edinburgh Chaplaincy Centre. It was a labyrinth constructed from mirrors. The white marble floor of the chapel became the path and the mirrors the 'fields' or edges of the path. As the walker moved along the path of the labyrinth they could see their reflection in the mirrors alongside them.

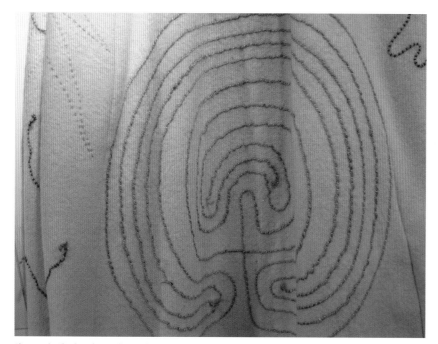

Shaman's Cloak Labyrinth, England.

Parks, gardens & country houses

Urban parks and gardens offer accessible places for community recreation and renewal. Since the millennium there have been an increasing number of labyrinths put into public and private parks and gardens.

Within the UK examples can be discovered in a variety of locations; two quite different labyrinths in parks in Milton Keynes, a millennium labyrinth in a small public garden in Whitehaven, a large 'Earth and Wildflower' labyrinth in Tapton Park, Chesterfield and the Edinburgh Labyrinth lying in eighteenth century gardens.

Increasingly, labyrinths are finding their way into the grounds of rural country houses such as the labyrinths in the grounds of both Mirehouse and Holker Hall in Cumbria. They are there for visitors to discover and walk.

In addition there are hotels offering an holistic 'well-being' experience including labyrinth walks, such as the Yoganature Centre for Health and WellBeing in Canterbury, Kent.

Holker Hall Labyrinth, Cumbria, England.

"I felt peace in my body and mind, which I have not felt for some time now. Thoughts stopped buzzing in my head and it felt like everything slotted into place. My life hasn't changed, but I feel stronger, revived and more able to deal with what I am facing."

Helen, Edinburgh Labyrinth

Cathedrals & churches

Labyrinths are ancient pathways for the human spirit. It is no surprise then that they are found not only by the ocean, in forests and on hillside plateaus, but also in cathedrals and churches. Because the medieval development of the labyrinth took place primarily within Christianity, the last millennium has seen waves of labyrinth construction in the floors, in the grounds and on the walls and ceilings of these buildings. In Hereford Cathedral the famous thirteenth century world map, the Mappa Mundi, is displayed for visitors. On the map the island of Crete has a drawing of an eleven-circuit medieval labyrinth.

In the UK, cathedrals such as Ely, Guildford and Norwich have permanent labyrinths as do a growing number of churches. These include the nineteenth century indoor labyrinths in Alkborough Church, Lincolnshire

and Itchen Stoke Church, Hampshire, and the more recent installations in Holy Trinity, North Ormesby, Polwarth Parish Church, Edinburgh, St John's Copthorne, West Sussex, St Michael's All Angels, Oxfordshire and St John's, Glastonbury, Somerset.

In other churches and cathedrals portable canvas labyrinths are in use on a regular basis or for particular events.

In all these settings the labyrinth is usually understood as a form of embodied prayer, a place of contemplation and pilgrimage. For some, to walk to the centre is to journey to one's own centre in Christ. Taking one step at a time symbolises the walker's relationship and journey of trust.

"Right at the depth of the human condition lies the longing for human presence, the silent desire for a communion…it is through the heart, in the depth of themselves, that human beings begin to grasp the mystery of faith. An inner life is developed step by step."

Br Roger of Taizé

Alkborough Church, England.

"Hope lights this space
where pilgrims come
seeking balance.

Barefoot we follow
the ancient pattern
guided by candles
incense and instinct.

United in our journey
our perspective
of one another changes
as the labyrinth's curves
take us towards
then away
sideways
then forwards,
travelling not to Jerusalem
but to the centre."

Key Proudlock

Chartres Cathedral Labyrinth, France.

St Lawrence Church, Rathmore, Ireland.

"Be still and know that I am God."

Psalm 46:10

"You will show me the path of life
  You will fill me with joy in your presence."

Ps 16:11

"What does the Lord require of you but to do justice,
  and to love kindness, and to walk humbly with your God?"

Micah 6:8

Hospices & hospitals

Labyrinths are appearing in hospitals and hospices such as Trinity Hospice, Blackpool, Pilgrims Hospice, Canterbury, North Tyneside General Hospital, Charis Integrated Cancer Care Centre, Cookstown, N Ireland and Maggie's Centre, Ninewells Hospital, Dundee.

There appears to be a growing recognition amongst some medical practitioners that patients, staff and visitors alike need quiet, safe spaces where they can go to process their feelings and thoughts when illness and death are close. Many institutions already provide chapels, sanctuaries or contemplation spaces. Labyrinths are yet another resource for support. Rebekah Clitherow of the Linden Centre, Trinity Hospice in Blackpool writes:

"At first sight the Linden Centre Labyrinth is often mistaken for a maze or whirlpool. Those living with serious illness or bereavement are often wary of walking into the labyrinth just as they fear the road ahead. However, when the courage is summoned and they walk that difficult path, especially in sight of someone else, clarity and comfort can be found. The path is often waterlogged or littered with sticks and stones but as they grow in awareness of their inner feelings they can overcome them and go forward. That person's journey is always a unique one, just as any outdoor labyrinth is different every day of the year but there is perhaps comfort in knowing that this is a path that has been and will be walked many times."

Linden Centre Labyrinth, Trinity Hospice, Blackpool, England.

"We are not capable of being alive in the present moment. We tend to postpone being alive to the future...now is not the moment to be alive. We may never be alive at all in our entire life. Therefore, the technique, if we have to speak of a technique, is to be in the present moment, to be aware that we are here and now, and the only moment to be alive is the present moment...this is the only moment that is real. To be here and now, and enjoy the present moment is our most important task."

Thich Nhat Hanh

Research is also underway to gather evidence about the effect of walking labyrinths on general stress reduction and health. Dr M. Kay Sandor of the University of Texas Medical Branch, School of Nursing, is keen to find out whether "walking the labyrinth may have stress reduction health benefits similar to a sitting meditation practice."

She worked with two groups of women on a two month walking programme. All participants reported work-related stress and/or caregiver stress at baseline.

One group walked the labyrinth, the other a regular walking track. Her working hypothesis was "Women who participate in a labyrinth walking program will show decreased serum cortisol levels, decreased behavioral levels of stress (perceived stress,

negative affect, anxiety, aggression, and depression), and increased positive affect and spiritual well-being when compared to women who participate in a track walking program." Research indicated that both groups showed a significant decrease in serum cortisol levels, however there were no significant differences between groups.

However, over time, women in the labyrinth walking group showed a significant decrease in anxiety and verbal aggression compared to the track walking group.

Practitioners who offer labyrinths within health settings are beginning to appreciate the way walking the labyrinth incorporates "body, mind and spirit in an integrative, holistic practice."

Ninewells Hospital, Dundee, Scotland.

Conferences & festivals

The labyrinth is becoming used as a space for stillness in busy conference settings, or at vast, noisy, summer festival events such as Greenbelt, held annually in Cheltenham, UK, or the Festival of Spirituality and Peace, one of the annual Edinburgh Festivals.

If there is no permanent labyrinth on site, portable labyrinths are laid down or simple labyrinths created for the duration of the event.

Greenbelt Festival Labyrinth, England.

"Something that took me by surprise...how the thoughts I had, suddenly received a totally new wording or expression that helped me see the issue in a different light."

Tampere conference workshop

"Reflective, restful – my mind was able to become peaceful and relaxed – simply 'being'."

Tampere conference workshop

Retreat, counselling & life coaching

There is a growing interest in placing labyrinths in retreat and spirituality centres such as Lendrick Lodge, The Bield, and Garden Cottage in Perthshire, Scotland, Shepherd's Dene in Northumberland, Holy Rood House, Thirsk, Scargill House, Kettlewell, England, St. Beuno's, North Wales and An Tobar in Co. Meath, Ireland.

In these settings walking the labyrinth may be part of a programme or more usually, the labyrinth is there for guests to use for personal reflection.

Labyrinths are increasingly used both by counselling services such as those in the Universities of Dundee, Edinburgh and Kent, and in places where life coaching is offered like The Burn, an educational centre in Glenesk, Scotland. They are seen as safe, containing, and facilitative spaces in which life issues can find focus and new insights be gained.

Garden Cottage Retreat and Spirituality Centre Labyrinth, Kilgraston, Scotland.

"...an intensely moving and reflective experience. There are moments of doubt and faith, joy and sorrow, love and fear, decision and indecision. Am I on the right path?"

Frank, Edinburgh Labyrinth Project

"Come away from the din. Come away to the quiet fields, over which the great sky stretches, and where, between us and the stars, there lies but silence; and there, in the stillness let us listen to the voice that is speaking within us."

Jerome K Jerome

The Burn Labyrinth, Glenesk, Scotland.

"Work is not always required…
There is such a thing as
sacred idleness, the
cultivation of which is
now fearfully neglected."

George MacDonald

"You have to slow
down near the centre."

Edinburgh Labyrinth Project

Schools

Labyrinths are being installed in schools, colleges and universities in many countries. The Head of Uyeasound Primary School on the island of Unst in Shetland writes this…

"This small island school is also known as the Rainbowlight school because of the large rainbow labyrinth that dominates the playground. The seven circuit classical labyrinth is a replica of a labyrinth introduced to Unst by Swedish fishermen in the late 19th and early parts of the 20th century. The labyrinth was used as a form of blessing before the men went to sea. Other examples of the labyrinth can be found around the Baltic.

We made the labyrinth in 2004 as part of a project to improve school grounds. It is 125 metres in and out of the labyrinth. Many of our pupils run around it up to 3 times a day or make up games using the circuits and colours. It helps us promote healthy living. We often use it as a meeting place or outdoor stage. It is a multifaith space for religious observance accepted by all major faiths.

This labyrinth is not only used by our pupils but also attracts many visitors to our playground. It is used by locals and visitors alike as a place to meditate and focus. It is also great fun."

There are several people writing resources for the use of labyrinths in schools and youth work.

See the resource section on page 96.

"Today was the first time I walked the labyrinth. I enjoyed the peacefulness…it really helped me unwind and be thankful. I will now come again. It's a wonderful place for my mind."

Joanne, age 14

Rainbowlight Labyrinth, Uyeasound Primary School, Shetland, Scotland. Photograph by Kate Coutts.

Colleges & universities

An increasing number of college and university faculties and support services throughout the UK are using the labyrinth to complement the standard academic approaches to individual and group learning and reflection.

The University of Kent is establishing creative spaces on campus to enhance teaching and learning. The use of portable canvas labyrinths and the creation of a permanent turf labyrinth is a significant part of this process. This follows the success of such labyrinth projects as those in Dundee and Edinburgh Universities.

In a culture that is predominantly book or computer based, the labyrinth offers institutions a unique space in which students and staff may explore non-prescriptive experiential and participatory learning. Walking the path offers the possibility of a freeing up of creative blocks and of focusing attention on the more subtle insights that arise in our imagination.

The Edinburgh Labyrinth, George Square Gardens, Edinburgh, Scotland.

"Take time out and tread the path of Scotland's only permanent [pavement] labyrinth. Situated in the northwest corner of George Square Gardens, The Edinburgh Labyrinth is a chance to slow down and still the mind. Not to be confused with a maze riddled with dizzying dead ends, labyrinths have only one clear path to follow, for when you need to shut out all distractions and take a moment to reflect. This 13th century design, based on the original at Chartres Cathedral in France, is the perfect way to unwind – going round and round in circles is finally a good thing!"

Claudia Monteiro & Owen O'Leary

"I find walking the labyrinth is excellent for being present… it is not possible to see the way ahead so the moment becomes more precious. The whole process definitely offers clarity and calm. What a relief!"

Anonymous, Edinburgh Labyrinth

"Slows one's life down."

Anonymous, Edinburgh Labyrinth

"It's a lovely experience coming back to walk the labyrinth after the holidays. Hadn't imagined that I'd miss it so dearly. It was, in a sense, the real holiday. I had felt free. I realised that in the last holidays I had tried to throw away the burden of work. But as the holidays went on I was more burdened with guilt of not doing any work. I had not managed to come back as refreshed as I had wanted. Now that I've had my real holiday I'm sure I can handle this term well."

Lai Ling, Edinburgh Labyrinth

Canterbury Labyrinth, University of Kent, England.

The University of Edinburgh Canvas Labyrinth, Scotland.

"Breathing out my worries as I walk the path in.
Opening to wisdom as I leave.
A simple white path, mirror to our deepest self.
Revealing what is there."

Edinburgh Labyrinth

"It gives me space to have an inner conversation, to find out what it is that is on my mind."

Edinburgh Labyrinth

"The path made me pause from the movements of my life, but also reminded me that spiritual and meditative mediums such as the labyrinth really are the important links in the chain of our life as a spiritual being.
I realised today that recently I have been a human being trying to live spiritually rather than a spiritual being leading, or living in, a human life.
Good to have a reminder."

Soraiya, Edinburgh Labyrinth

Creating labyrinths –
classical & medieval

Saltburn Beach Labyrinth, England. Photograph by Clare Blakey.

"You want a place where you can be serene,
that will let you contemplate and connect
two consecutive thoughts,
or that if need be,
can stir you up,
as you were made to be stirred up,
until you blend with the wind
and water and earth
you almost forgot you came from."

Anonymous

Classical seven-circuit labyrinth

There are two archetypal labyrinth patterns, the ancient classical seven-circuit and the eleven-circuit medieval. Variations on these two basic patterns exist. For the purposes of this book I will limit my descriptions of creating your own labyrinth to the classical and medieval.

For at least 4000 years it seems that people throughout the world have been using much the same method of creating a seven-circuit classical labyrinth as we do today. Whether scratching a labyrinth onto a cave wall, painting one on a ceramic pot or laying one out in stones near the ocean, the process is the same.

1   Draw out a simple square cross. Within each quadrant of the cross shape you add a corner angle. At the four corners of the resulting imagined square place a dot.

2   Beginning at the top of the vertical line of the centre cross, draw an arc connecting it to the top of the line to the right of the cross. This forms a central space within the labyrinth design.

3   Join the vertical line, left of the centre cross, with the top right-hand dot.

4   Connect the top left-hand dot to the horizontal line of the top right–hand corner angle by a longer arc.

5-8   Then, systematically starting at each remaining free line and dot, work down the left-hand side of the emerging pattern, drawing longer and longer arcs connecting to the next available line or dot down the length of the right-hand side.

9   Finally, join the vertical line of the bottom left-hand corner angle to the base of the vertical cross with a concluding encompassing arc. The space between each arc would form the path of the labyrinth.

The ancient classical design is a wonderful design to use if you want to create a simple labyrinth to walk. It can be made out of the natural materials you find around you. You just need to make sure that as you lay the first cross and corner angles the distance between the lines, and thus the subsequent arcs, will offer a path which is wide enough to walk comfortably.

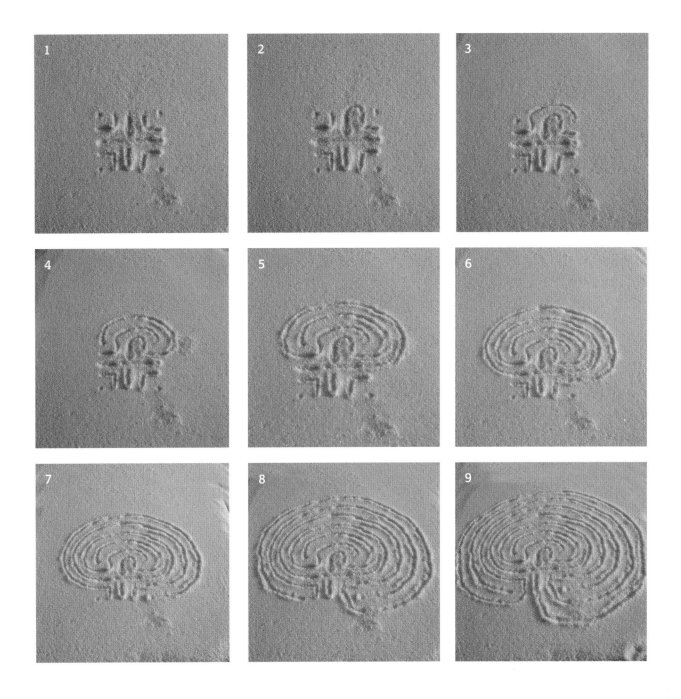

Wanting a labyrinth to walk during an autumn day of reflection we set about gathering fallen leaves into a large pile. Then, working purely by eye, we laid out the central cross, angles and corner dots of a classic seven-circuit labyrinth. Within half an hour we had completed the path of a beautiful golden leafed labyrinth, which we walked as dusk fell.

One of the great things about creating labyrinths is that with a little ingenuity you can make them out of materials that are around you.

It took just a few hours to collect seaweed and lay out a labyrinth on the Isle of Lismore, Scotland.

"God help us to live slowly
to move simply
to look softly
to allow emptiness
to let the heart create for us."

Michael Leunig

Manas's Labyrinth, Isle of Lismore, Scotland.

"Here are words written down –
footprints on the sand,
cloud formations.

Tomorrow
I'll be gone."

Thich Nhat Hanh

Ganges Labyrinth, India.

I was sailing down the Ganges in central
India, sleeping each night on the shoreline
or sandbanks. One morning I woke early
with a strong desire to walk a labyrinth
in memory of my uncle who had died
suddenly whilst I had been travelling.

I found a long, sturdy stick and drew
out the shape of a classical labyrinth in
the sand fairly close to the water's edge.
As the sun rose over the river I began
my celebration of his life. I walked into
the labyrinth, quietly letting out my
grief. In the centre I remembered, and
gave thanks for him, then turned to
walk the return path with the beginning
of a new sense of peace.

A friend was travelling to Korea for a conference. She wanted to take a portable labyrinth with her to provide a place of stillness and reflection for the many delegates. A canvas medieval labyrinth was too large and heavy for her to transport. Over the course of a few weeks a colleague and I sourced some light calico and sewed it together in strips to make one large piece of cloth. We stretched it out on a wooden hall floor and, using a huge number of torn off scraps of newspaper, laid out the classical seven-circuit pattern on the cloth.

Where each scrap of paper lay we marked the cloth with a dot of paint, then collected up the paper as we dotted our way round the whole pattern. A small group of students and staff joined us in transforming each dot into a larger painted pebble shape adding our intentions as we painted.

By the end of the evening a beautiful, living, hand-painted 'pebble labyrinth' was ready for its long journey ahead.

"May the blessing of God go before you.
May her grace and peace abound.
May her spirit live within you.
May her love wrap you round.
May her blessing remain with you always.
May you walk on holy ground."

Miriam Therese Winter

Painted 'Pebble Labyrinth', University of Edinburgh, Scotland.

On the lower slopes of Scargill House estate, in Wharfedale, Yorkshire, close to the remains of an Iron Age Brigante Roundhouse, you can find a 29' classic seven-circuit limestone labyrinth. It was built in 2005 in a clearing under trees out of roughly 600 pieces of local white limestone which had been gathered from a disused dry stone wall nearby.

It took nine people just one morning to build. We had a wheelbarrow and plenty of pairs of garden gloves!

To be certain that it would fit the site one of the team had previously worked out the geometry of the labyrinth on paper. Using coloured string and measuring canes the dimensions were transferred to the ground. Then the lines of the labyrinth were laid down lightly with the sort of paint you use to spray onto the grass of sports fields. By coffee time the pattern of the labyrinth lay before us in the grass.

The final task of the morning was to fetch the pieces of limestone and place them along the painted lines to form the permanent 'fields' or boundaries of the labyrinth's path. It was a wonderful, almost meditative experience.

In just under an hour the team laid all 600 stones and the Scargill Labyrinth had come into existence.

You might want to visit www. labyrinthsociety.org/make-a-labyrinth to discover more about the geometry of laying out a permanent seven-circuit classical labyrinth.

Scargill Labyrinth Build

It was enchanting.
We moved in quietness,
with intent and love.
The final stone closing
the circle of our joy.

Walking Blessing

That each step
may be a shedding.
That you will let yourself
become lost.
That when it looks
like you're going backwards,

you may be making progress.
That progress is not the goal anyway,
but presence
to the feel of the path on your skin,
to the way it reshapes you
in each place it makes contact,

to the way you cannot see it
until the moment you have stepped out.

Jan Richardson

Scargill Labyrinth, Kettlewell, England.

Medieval eleven-circuit labyrinth

The medieval design is felt by many to be a more balancing path to walk. Walkers find themselves turning alternately to the left then to the right at most of the thirty-four turns throughout the walk to the centre. There is a sense also that the complexity of the path ahead is unreadable to the walker, which thus allows the mind to cease racing ahead and settle the body to take one step at a time, trusting the path to reveal itself without need for thought.

However, the medieval design is a more complex pattern than the classical to replicate. It demands a little more skill in laying it out. You might want to try to make one after you have had some success with the classical design.

There are several on-line sites which offer help in setting out a medieval, eleven-circuit labyrinth. You might want to check out a resource such as www.labyrinthsociety.org/make-a-labyrinth.

This next section highlights medieval labyrinths made out of different materials.

"Stand at the crossroads and look and ask for ancient paths, where the good way lies; and walk in it, and find rest for your souls."
Jeremiah 6:16

Alkborough Village, England.

Hand-painted canvas labyrinths are lovely to walk. They are a soft and natural fibre for your feet. You can paint your own or there are several artists and companies who produce them to a high standard. The most popular design is a replica of the 800 year-old stone labyrinth in the floor of Chartres Cathedral in France.

These canvases are portable and usually arrive in a wheeled plastic container. They have presented the first opportunity of walking a labyrinth to many thousands of people across the planet.

You can purchase canvas labyrinths through www.veriditas.org or for UK based possibilities visit - www.diwilliams.com

University of Edinburgh Canvas Labyrinth, Scotland.

The Journey Prayer

"God, bless the pathway on which I go.
 God, bless the earth that is beneath my sole;
 Bless, O God, and give to me Thy love..."

From the Carmina Gadelica

A labyrinth path can be made out of turf such as Julian's Bower in the village of Alkborough, North Lincolnshire. It is one of only eight surviving historical turf labyrinths in England. The other seven labyrinths are at Breamore, Dalby, Hilton, Saffron Walden, Somerton, Winchester and Wing.

A turf labyrinth is constructed by cutting away the ground with metal tools to leave raised strips of turf and clean soil, gravel or sandy trenches a few inches below the level of the remaining turf. In most constructions the turf becomes the path to the centre. In some cases it is possible to design the labyrinth to use the trench rather than the turf as the path.

The eight historical turf labyrinths in England are looked after well enough for people to walk them. Creating a new turf labyrinth needs to take into account the future maintenance of path and 'fields'.

Hilton Turf Labyrinth, England

Edinburgh
labyrinth project

The Edinburgh Labyrinth was the first permanent stone pavement labyrinth built in Scotland.

From 2001 the University of Edinburgh regularly used a Chartres-design canvas for staff and students to walk.

To develop the project we needed to install a labyrinth that would be much more accessible to the University and Edinburgh community. In 2004 the Development Trust of the University granted the University Chaplaincy the funding to take the lead in the construction of this innovative labyrinth project.

Working with the university architect, city planning, a land artist and a landscaping company, the building of the labyrinth began in 2004 in the peaceful setting of the 18th century George Square Gardens in Edinburgh's Old Town. It was opened in 2005.

"Beannachd air an àite seo
Eadar craobh is clach is feur.
Beannachd air gach duin' a thig
Gum faigh iad fois is sàmhchair ann.
Blessings on this place where we stand
between tree and stone and grass.
Blessings on all who walk this path
that they may find here peace and quietness."

Catriona Mackie

The Edinburgh Labyrinth, World Wide Labyrinth Day 2009, Scotland.

Finger labyrinth

Finger labyrinths have a special place in the history and contemporary use of labyrinths. The 6th century Hollywood Stone classical labyrinth discovered in 1908 in County Wicklow, Ireland and the 10th century medieval design carved into the wall of the bell tower of Lucca Cathedral in Italy are examples of labyrinths small enough to trace with a finger. The latter is often used before entering the cathedral.

These days they are readily available in wood, ceramic, glass, plastic, sand and cloth. You can even trace one on-line. They are used for personal reflection particularly when it is not possible to walk a larger labyrinth.

Tracing a labyrinth with your finger gives you a moment to stop what you are doing. Consciously bring yourself into the present moment and then slowly follow the path with your finger. As in walking a labyrinth on the ground, shed any unnecessary preoccupations on the journey to the centre. When you reach the centre take a moment to experience it as a place of resting and receiving. When you are ready, trace your journey back along the path aware of any insights, feelings or thoughts that you may want to reflect on a little more.

You may find it interesting to trace the path using your non-dominant hand or with closed eyes. Why not try tracing the path on the labyrinth opposite.

"O angel guardian of my right hand,
...Guide thou my step in gap and pit..."

From the Carmina Gadelica

Finger labyrinth.

Facilitating labyrinths

Facilitating walks

If you have the use of a portable or permanent labyrinth you may want to introduce walking the labyrinth to other people.

People come across labyrinths and walk them without the help of prior information or the presence of someone who knows about the labyrinth. That was my experience in discovering my first labyrinth on the coast of South Wales. Although I remember that walk with joy, I didn't know it was a labyrinth I was walking nor did I realise what such a space might offer.

My second encounter with a labyrinth was qualitatively different. Walking a facilitated labyrinth made a significant difference for me. Before we walked, the facilitator shared a basic presentation about labyrinths. He gave the group simple, practical advice about walking the path alongside others. He encouraged us to walk with an open mind and heart rather than with particular expectations. The facilitator's knowledgeable and supportive approach helped me to let go of my natural cynicism. I discovered that I was able to engage more fully in my experience of the walk. For me that second labyrinth walk became a memorable occasion of connection, learning and transformation.

Leading a labyrinth walk or workshop that offers people a similarly supportive and engaging setting is an art. To do it well takes sensitivity and skill. The ideal way to begin is to train as a Labyrinth Facilitator with a reputable organisation. A good training course should cover areas such as the origin, history and contemporary development of labyrinths, basic construction issues and the use of labyrinths in different settings. It should address labyrinth event design and how to adapt a pre-walk presentation to fit the particular context in which you are working.

If an opportunity to facilitate a labyrinth occurs before you have embarked on training, the following basic pointers should be helpful. If at all possible plan and carry out the event with others. As far as you can, prepare the labyrinth space to offer a safe, accessible, welcoming and peaceful environment for participants. You may want to think about providing non-intrusive background music or offering a candlelit walk.

If you are using a portable labyrinth indoors, make sure it fits into the allotted venue space. Ideally, there should be room to spare around the outside of the labyrinth. This makes for ease of movement at the entrance to the path and space for reflection, rest and witnessing the walk of others.

Facilitated open walk.

Decide what further resources you might want available. I have found it helpful to provide a simple leaflet about labyrinths for participants to read before walking, as well as a range of books about labyrinths for them to browse or purchase. If you would like to help walkers process the experience of their walk, then the provision of journaling and art materials and a comment book may be valuable. You may want to add a finger labyrinth (particularly useful for someone who finds walking the path physically difficult), a contact list and, depending on the situation, a donation bowl!

Think about the context in which you are offering the labyrinth and prepare a short presentation to introduce walkers to the labyrinth. You will find the Introduction to this book (pages 20-23) will give you an idea of what to include in your talk. Keep it short and be sure to offer practical information about walking the path alongside others. When you are ready to open the labyrinth, stand near the entrance so that you can quietly regulate the spacing of those entering the path. This helps keep the labyrinth

from getting overcrowded and ensures walkers have a more spacious experience. It sometimes helps to suggest that folk take time for personal preparation before they enter the labyrinth. This helps stagger the entry of walkers quite naturally and may often help to deepen the experience of the subsequent walk. Throughout the period the labyrinth is open for walking, be gently attentive to what is happening on the path and in the room or setting around the labyrinth. Be calm and 'hold' the stillness with a non-anxious presence.

A few years ago I helped facilitate a labyrinth at a huge summer festival. It took our small team nearly two days and a lot of soapy water to transform a dark, dirty and smelly bar into an inviting and peaceful space. We created restful places near to the labyrinth where people could sit or lie on cushions and rugs and decompress a little. We set up an area with candles for people to light by way of intention or prayer. There were several small tables with paper, coloured pens and comment books. These became well used places for processing feelings and

thoughts after walking the labyrinth. The labyrinth was open about nine or ten hours each day. Over the three days we welcomed more than 2000 adults and children onto the path. There was an almost constant stream of people wanting to walk. With three trained facilitators and several volunteers on the team we were able to ensure a trained person was almost always present to facilitate the entrance of walkers onto the path. Other team members welcomed people at the door and dealt with practical issues. Some members of the team were skilled at keeping a quiet eye out for anyone who seemed to connect with a deep emotion or maybe wished to talk about their experience. There was always someone to relieve a team colleague of their particular task so that they could get a refreshment or lunch break. The huge interest in walking the labyrinth meant the team's work was demanding. It was also a delight. Providing an environment in which people of all ages could drop into a place of stillness and maybe experience something of timely significance was wonderful for the team to participate in.

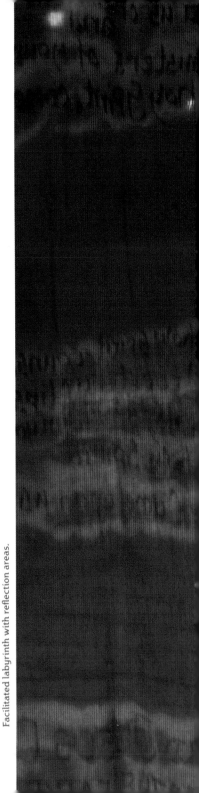

Facilitated labyrinth with reflection areas.

Facilitator training

Should you wish to develop your understanding of labyrinths and your skill in leading open walks or workshops I encourage you to look out for labyrinth workshops you can attend or think about helping as a volunteer in a local labyrinth project. If you are serious about developing your work with labyrinths then apply to go on a Labyrinth Facilitator Training course. You will find yourself training alongside people who are using labyrinths in a variety of contexts. Learning with others is a great way to share and deepen experience and to forge a sense of being part of a world-wide labyrinth community.

Veriditas, a US based organisation dedicated to introducing people to the labyrinth world-wide, offers "the most comprehensive labyrinth facilitator training available." Their UK training programme was launched in 2010. The author is the first Veriditas Master Teacher in the UK and Ireland.

For information about training in the UK and wider visit www.veriditas.org and www.diwilliams.com.

"Wonderful, nourishing, inspiring...
I am raring to go."

Facilitator Training participant

Lyveden Labyrinth: contemporary mowed labyrinth on site of ancient turf labyrinth, rediscovered 2010, Lyveden, England: Copyright National Trust.

Websites and suggested reading

For further information, visit:

www.diwilliams.com
www.veriditas.org
www.labyrinthsociety.org
www.labyrinth.ed.ac.uk
www.labyrinthos.co.uk
www.labyrinthuk.org

You will find a link to the world-wide labyrinth locator at most of these sites. There you can search for the labyrinth nearest to where you live or where you are visiting.

If you would like to read more about labyrinths, here are some suggested titles.

Artress, Lauren. (1995) Walking a Sacred Path: Rediscovering the Labyrinth as a Sacred Tool. New York: Riverhead Books.

Artress, Lauren. (2006) The Sacred Path Companion.New York: Riverhead Books.

Thanks

Clare – for your caring support throughout this project.

Pauline – for inspiration when the path seemed blocked .

Janet – Anam Cara.

Veriditas – and the world-wide labyrinth community for friendship on the journey.

￢ nes – for a beautiful design.

Buchanan, Jim. (2007) Labyrinths for the Spirit. London: Gaia Books.

Geoffrion, Jill Kimberly Hartwell. (1999) Praying the Labyrinth: A Journal for Spiritual Exploration. Cleveland, OH: Pilgrim Press.

Geoffrion, Jill Kimberly Hartwell. (2000) Living the Labyrinth: 101 Paths to a Deeper Connection with the Sacred. Cleveland, OH: Pilgrim Press.

Kern, Hermann. (2000) Through the Labyrinth: Designs and Meanings over 5,000 Years. New York: Prestel Press.

McCarthy, Marge. (2007) Kids on the Path: School Labyrinth Guide. Sante Fe: Labyrinth Resource Group.

Sands, Helen Raphael. (2000) Labyrinth: Pathway to Meditation and Healing. London: Gaia Books.

Saward, Jeff. (2003) Labyrinths & Mazes: A Complete Guide to magical Paths of the World. London: Gaia Books.

Sources

Grateful acknowledgement is made to the following publishers and individuals for material used in Labyrinth – landscape of the soul. Should any acknowledgements be less than accurate, I will be happy to make any adjustments in any subsequent editions of this book.

Anon, from The Place No One Knew in Winds from the Wilderness, p132, © Outward Bound Canada 1982

Brother Roger of Taizé, Trust on Earth p 5 © Atelier et Presses de Taizé, 71250 Taizé Community, France 2002

Carmina Gadelica collected by Alexander Carmichael, Edited by CJ Moore © Edinburgh Floris Books 1994, 2001

Chitty, Lynne, 'The Labyrinth' in Tracing the Labyrinth, Poems from Gloucester Cathedral, by Lynne Chitty © Dean and Chapter of Gloucester Cathedral 2002

Jerome, Jerome K, Diary of a Pilgrimage (and Six Essays), p323 © New York, H Holt 1891

LeGuin, Ursula K, from The Farthest Shore in Winds from the Wilderness, p141, © Outward Bound Canada 1982

Leunig, Michael, The Common Prayer, © Oxford, Lion Publishing 1997

Leunig, Michael, The Prayer Tree, © Oxford, Lion Publishing 1997

Lindbergh, Anne Morrow, from Gift from the Sea in Winds from the Wilderness, p133, © Outward Bound Canada 1982

MacDonald, George, George MacDonald: An Anthology by CS Lewis, p109, published by Macmillan 1947

Monterio, Claudia & O'Leary, Owen, The Locals' Guide to Edinburgh, p105 © Edinburgh, Word of Mouth Travels Ltd 2007

Proudlock, Key, from Pointing at Rainbows, a third collection of poems from women writers in Fife; compiled and edited by Lillian King; p30 © Kelty, Windfall Books 2000

"Walking Blessing" from In Wisdom's Path: Discovering the Sacred in Every Season © Jan L. Richardson. www.janrichardson.com Used by permission of the author.

Thich Nhat Hanh, p163 Reprinted from Stepping into Freedom: An Introduction to Buddhist Monastic Training, (1997) by Thich Nhat Hanh with permission of Parallax Press, Berkeley, California. www.parallax.org

Thich Nhat Hanh, p41 Reprinted from Our Appointment with Life: Discourse on Living Happily in the Present Moment (1990) by Thich Nhat Hanh with permission of Parallax Press, Berkeley, California. www.parallax.org

Thich Nhat Hanh, p26 Reprinted from Being Peace, (1987, 2005) by Thich Nhat Hanh with permission of Parallax Press, Berkeley, California. www.parallax.org

Thich Nhat Hanh, p51 Reprinted from Call Me by My True Names: The Collected Poems of Thich Nhat Hanh (1999) by Thich Nhat Hanh with permission of Parallax Press, Berkeley, California. www.parallax.org

Winter, Miriam Therese, Blessing Song, © Hartford, Medical Mission Sisters, 1987